D1076380

SPEED BOAT

Mark Beyer

Children's Press
A Division of Grolier Publishing
New York / London / Hong Kong / Sydney
Danbury, Connecticut

Book Design: Michael DeLisio
Contributing Editor: Jeri Cipriano
Photo Credits: Cover, pp. 4, 12, 26, 31, © Indexstock; pp. 6, 9, 22, 28, 32, 35, 40 © Neil Rabinowitz/Corbis; p. 15 © AP/Wide World Photos/Andy Newman; p. 16 © Kevin Fleming/Corbis; p. 19 © AP/Wide World Photos/Jay Drawns; p. 20 AP/Wide World Photos/ Ernest Lambert; p. 25 © AP/Wide World Photos/Rod Millington; p. 36 © AP/Wide World Photos/Seth Rossman; p. 39 © Corbis

Visit Children's Press on the Internet at:
http://publishing.grolier.com

Library of Congress Cataloging-in-Publication Data

Beyer, Mark.
  Speed boat / by Mark Beyer.
  p. cm. — (Built for speed)
  Includes bibliographical references and index.
  ISBN 0-516-23162-6 (lib. bdg.) — ISBN 0-516-23265-7 (pbk.)
  1. Motorboats—Juvenile literature. [1. Motorboats.] I. Title: Speedboat. II. Title. III. Built for speed

GV835 .B49 2000
797.1'25—dc21

                                                    00-063897

CONTENTS

INTRODUCTION

Going fast is an exciting feeling. People drive fast cars. People ride fast on bicycles. People race on foot and in machines.

Boat racing has been around ever since there were boats to paddle. When engines were used to power boats, racing became faster and more exciting. Speed is just one part of racing. To be a powerboat champion, you have to drive better than the other racers.

Today, men and women race boats that have huge engines. Some of these engines have the pulling power of a thousand horses. High-speed boats travel as fast as 220 miles (354 km) per hour. However, racing on the water is not just about speed. These power-boats must race around a track, just the way

Powerboats are the fastest things on the water.

A hydroplane speeds past a buoy on a racecourse.

cars do in auto racing. Floating markers called buoys mark the racetrack. The boats move up to the starting line. A light flashes to start the race. POW! The roar of twenty powerful engines blasts across the shores. The spray of water shoots up behind the boats. The crowd watches as the boats speed past. The race has begun!

POWERBOATS
and Racing Classes

Many different types of boats are used for powerboat racing. Some racing boats are only 9 feet (2.7 m) long. These small boats travel at speeds up to 95 miles (153 km) per hour. There are also Offshore racing boats. These boats race on ocean waters. Offshore boats can be up to 48 feet (14.5 m) long. Offshore powerboats have one, two, or three engines. They race at 150 miles (241.5 km) per hour over ocean waves.

Offshore powerboats are not for the small boat racer. They can cost hundreds of thousands of dollars!

THE AMERICAN POWER BOAT ASSOCIATION (APBA)

Any two people who have boats can race down a river. But to be crowned a champion, you must belong to a racing group. The American Power Boat Association (APBA) sponsors races across the country. There are sixteen different regions of APBA racing. On any weekend, there are hundreds of races run in many different states.

Powerboat Racing Categories

The APBA has twelve categories of powerboat racing. The categories have to do with boat types and engine size. Some boats have inboard engines. Inboard engines are placed inside boats and beneath a cover. Inboard engines can be near the center or back of the boat. A metal bar called a shaft connects the engine to the propeller. The propeller spins around and pushes the boat across the water.

These powerboats are in fierce competition at the Seafare race.

Other boats have outboard engines. Outboard engines sit on the back of the boat. The bottom part of the engine holds the propeller. The propeller sits in the water.

Powerboat Racing Classes

Within each category of boat racing, there is also a class, or type of boat or motor. Some classes of racing boats are determined by the size of the motor used in the boat. The hull (boat body) and the engine size determine other classes. Powerboats have V-hulls, flat-bottom hulls, twin hulls (catamarans), and hydroplanes.

This book does not cover every category and class of powerboat. Instead it focuses on some of the more popular types of powerboats and racing events.

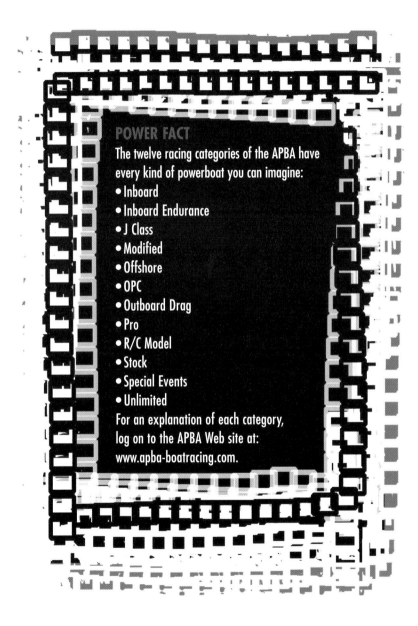

POWER FACT

The twelve racing categories of the APBA have every kind of powerboat you can imagine:

- Inboard
- Inboard Endurance
- J Class
- Modified
- Offshore
- OPC
- Outboard Drag
- Pro
- R/C Model
- Stock
- Special Events
- Unlimited

For an explanation of each category, log on to the APBA Web site at: www.apba-boatracing.com.

INBOARD
Powerboats

Inboard powerboats use automobile engines that are specially designed for boats. Inboard powerboat racing is classified by the boat's motor size and hull design. There are fourteen different classes of Inboard powerboat racing. The Flatbottom Runabout class boats use a flat bottom and a small engine. The high-speed Hydroplane class boats have engines that are 500 cubic inches (.008 m³).

FLATBOTTOM RUNABOUT CLASSES

Runabouts come in different lengths, but the minimum length is 9 feet (2.7 m). They travel at speeds from 80 miles (129 km) per hour to more than 140 miles (225 km) per hour. Runabouts are very stable on the water. They

Flatbottom Runabouts, such as the one shown here, are very stable on the water.

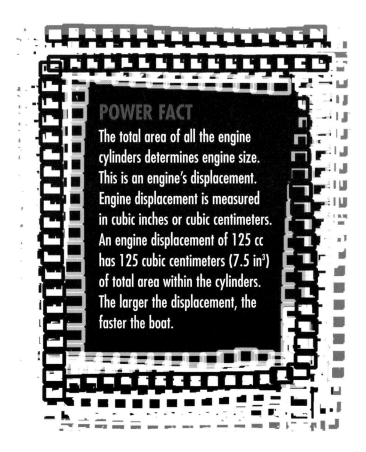

POWER FACT

The total area of all the engine cylinders determines engine size. This is an engine's displacement. Engine displacement is measured in cubic inches or cubic centimeters. An engine displacement of 125 cc has 125 cubic centimeters (7.5 in^3) of total area within the cylinders. The larger the displacement, the faster the boat.

can make a ninety-degree turn at more than 90 miles (145 km) per hour. This kind of racing allows boats to race close together. Fast boats racing side by side make an exciting race for fans to watch!

Sometimes the only part of a hydroplane boat that touches the water is the propeller!

Engine Size

Runabouts race using different engine sizes. The class of Runabout is determined by its engine size. The engines range from 7.5 cubic inches (123 cm³) to 69 cubic inches (.001 m³). The larger the engine, the faster the boat. Also, the larger the engine, the longer the boat.

Using engines and boats of equal size and length, the difference in winning and losing is in driving ability. Powerboat racing drivers know their engines and their boats. They know when to run an engine at maximum speed. They also know when to slow down for a turn. Winning a race is often the result of how a driver runs his engine.

Hull Shape and Handling

Runabouts have a flat bottom. The boat sits on two long hulls about 6 feet (1.8 m) apart. The hulls rest in the water and keep most of the boat out of the water. Only a few inches of the hull and the engine propeller sit in the water. Air passes below the boat, but not enough to lift the boat off the water. A Runabout's design is specially made for high-speed turns.

Flatbottom Runabout powerboats race around a buoyed track. Some races are three laps around a one-mile course. Other races are four laps around a three-quarter-mile course. The races are short. But the action on the water is fast and furious!

HYDROPLANE CLASSES

Hydroplane boats are specially designed to sit atop two curved hulls. These hulls sit higher in the water than the Runabouts. Hydroplane hull designs allow air to flow under the boat. This trapped air lifts the boat so that it runs just above the water's surface at top speed. Sometimes the only part of the boat touching the water is the propeller!

Engines and Classes

Hydroplane boats fall into classes depending on their engine size. Inboard Hydroplane power-boats use gasoline-powered automobile engines. These engines are modified for use in a boat. Some of the popular car engines used in Hydroplane boats are Ford, Plymouth, and

BMW. Engine sizes range from 246 cubic inches (.004 m³) to unlimited size. Inboard Hydroplane boat speeds range from 105 to 170 miles (169 to 274 km) per hour.

DRIVING A HYDROPLANE

Driving a boat in a group that is racing around a track at 130 miles (209 km) per hour is tricky. The spray other boats give off during a turn can hit like a sudden rainstorm!

Still more dangerous is the hydroplaning action of the boats during a race. The cushion of air that the boats ride on can make driving tricky. If there's too much air, the boat could float into the air and flip. But if there's suddenly no air beneath the boat, the nose can dive into the water.

Hydroplane races usually run two heats (elimination rounds) of three laps each. The Hydroplanes run counterclockwise around a buoyed track. The driver uses a side fin to

An Unlimited Hydroplane flips as it catches air from the spray of another boat during the finals of the General Motors Cup.

turn the Hydroplane boat in a level position. Hydroplane powerboats run well and fast on smooth water. If there are calm winds, the water is smooth. If it's windy, the water gets choppy. Choppy water makes Hydroplane racing rough and dangerous. At high speeds, choppy water kicks the front of the boat into the air. If the front end gets too high, the boat will flip backwards. But damage to boats is rare. Racers really know their boats. They

Here, a driver loses control as his boat becomes airborne.

understand how certain speeds affect boats. They know the conditions of the racetrack. Racers have no wish to harm themselves or to wreck expensive boats.

Offshore and Drag-racing
POWERBOATS

OFFSHORE

Offshore boats are the "big daddies" of power-boat racing. They must be big because they race on the ocean. Ocean waves and swells can be 6 to 10 feet (1.8 to 3 m) high. A small nine-foot runabout traveling at 120 miles (193 km) per hour could flip. A hydroplane power-boat might dive into the side of a wave.

Length and Hull Type

Offshore boat lengths range from 24 to 48 feet (7.3 to 14.5 m). There are two types of Offshore powerboat hulls: V and twin (catamarans). The V-hulls are wide above water and sharply point-ed below water. This gives them their "V" shape. Catamaran hulls have two narrow V-hulls that

allow air to pass below the boat. Some racers say V boats handle better on ocean waters. Other racers say catamarans are faster. It all depends on which racing team you ask.

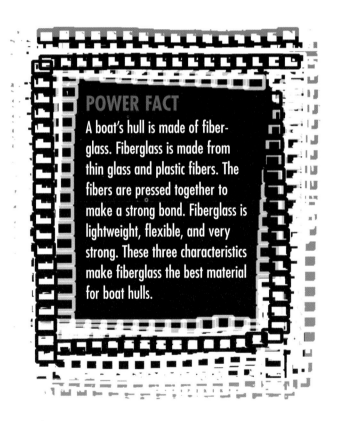

POWER FACT

A boat's hull is made of fiberglass. Fiberglass is made from thin glass and plastic fibers. The fibers are pressed together to make a strong bond. Fiberglass is lightweight, flexible, and very strong. These three characteristics make fiberglass the best material for boat hulls.

Some racers think that boats with V-hulls, like this one, handle better.

Engines

Offshore boats have either inboard or outboard engines. Some Offshore boats have one engine although others may have two or three engines. The number of engines, the size of the engines, and the size of the boats determine each class of Offshore racing. There are more than fourteen different Offshore racing classes. Engine size ranges from 375 cubic inches (.006 m³) to more than 1,400 cubic inches (.023 m³). Offshore boats can reach speeds of 150 miles (241.5 km) per hour. These boats can launch off ocean waves and get airborne—engine and all!

At the Races

Offshore powerboat races are long. They sometimes last for almost 2 hours. They cover more than 160 miles (257.5 km) of sea. The boats race around a series of buoys. Offshore boats have two crew members. One person

Offshore boats can launch off ocean waves and get airborne!

controls the speed. The other person pilots (steers) the boat. Offshore races require speed, driving skill, and endurance.

OUTBOARD DRAG RACING

Drag racing is something people think only cars do. Two cars line up and race down a quarter-mile (.4 km) track to the finish line. Boats can drag race, as well.

A production boat is used for water-skiing.

Racing Classes

The APBA has twelve classes of Outboard drag racing. Four of these classes allow everyday boaters to race their boats. As long as two boats are of equal length and engine size, they can enter a race. These four drag-race classes make up the Entry Level Sportsman Classes.

All four Sportsman classes use production boats (boats bought from a showroom dealer). These boats are the same as those you see on any lake or river. Some people use them for fishing or water-skiing during the week. On weekends, though, they take them to the races. The difference between the showroom boat and a drag-racing boat is in the engine. The drag-racing boat engine is changed to be more powerful. The more powerful a boat's engine is, the faster the boat can pick up speed. Getting the boat up to top speed quickly is the difference between winning and losing a drag race.

The kind of engine change determines the class in which the boat is placed. More engine changes mean a higher racing class. Some racing classes only allow engine changes that are made using parts that you can buy at the local auto parts store.

The other eight classes of drag racing are for professionals. These people bring high-tech boats to race. These drag-racing boats have 300 horsepower engines. They can reach speeds of 100 miles (161 km) per hour on a quarter-mile (.4 km) track. Most of the boats still have hulls from boats bought in a showroom. However, the engines have been turned into racing machines. Their speed across the water makes for exciting racing!

UNLIMITED
Hydroplanes

The Unlimited Hydroplanes are the fastest boats in the world. These boats look like spacecrafts on the water. They use jet engines to power them. Unlimited is the most popular powerboat racing category today.

A JET ON WATER

All hydroplane boats travel just above the water at top speed. But Unlimited Hydroplanes use turbine jet engines to power them. When hydroplaning, often no part of the boat touches the water. The boat actually flies just above the water. The Unlimited turbine jet engine can drive the boat 220 miles (354 km) per hour!

Danger exists all around at such high speeds. Winds can force the boat to flip.

Unlimited Hydroplanes use jet engines, such as this one, to power them.

Waves and jet wash (the rush of wind made by another boat's jet engine) also can cause flips. Boats can crash together while racing. Also, drivers can lose control of their boats.

Jet Engine Power

The Unlimited's jet engine is sealed in a compartment behind the pilot. A jet engine is a turbine engine. A turbine is a fan that spins at high speed. The fan pulls air from the front of the engine and pushes it out the back to give the boat power. The higher the turbine speed, the more power and speed for the boat. During a race, Unlimited Hydroplane boats can average lap speeds of more than 160 miles (257.5 km) per hour.

Designed for Speed and Safety

Unlimited Hydroplanes must be designed carefully to protect both the pilots and the boats. Unlimiteds are designed using computers. This high-tech designing makes them more aerodynamic, which means they can move through air more easily. A more aerodynamic boat is safer at higher speeds. The boat acts like a wing as it knifes through the air. If the boat is in the correct position, it stays in place. If the boat is out of position, it

Engineers use computers to design Unlimited Hydroplanes.

becomes dangerous for the driver and other racers. That is why an Unlimited has two wings on the back of the boat. These are tail wings that stand at an angle. They steer the

boat around the racecourse. The wings also help to keep the boat steady as it flies across the water.

Unlimited Hydroplanes are made of fiberglass. They are longer, wider, and heavier than the Inboard Hydroplane boats. Unlimiteds have to be larger to carry their jet engines safely.

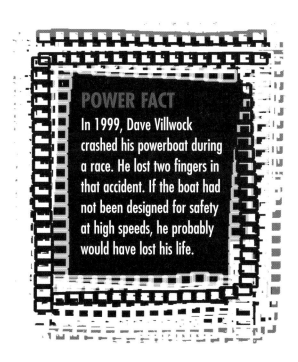

POWER FACT

In 1999, Dave Villwock crashed his powerboat during a race. He lost two fingers in that accident. If the boat had not been designed for safety at high speeds, he probably would have lost his life.

Unlimiteds have to be larger than Inboard boats to carry jet engines safely.

Unlimited Hydroplanes are nearly 20 feet (6 m) long and 8 feet (2.5 m) wide. They sit low on the water. This is their profile. This "low profile" allows the boat to make tighter turns at higher speeds without danger of flipping.

THE PILOT AND COCKPIT

The pilot of an Unlimited Hydroplane sits in a sealed space called the cockpit. The cockpit is a lot like a jet fighter cockpit. It is small and cramped. The cockpit has a steering wheel and a throttle to adjust the speed. It also has dials that tell the pilot how the engine is performing.

The windshield dome that shields the pilot from wind is made of a special plastic. This is the same plastic that is used for jet fighter cockpits. It cannot shatter if it is struck by an object. The dome protects the pilot from the rush of air that hits the boat at top speed. If the boat crashes, the pilot is safe from danger.

The pilot of an Unlimited Hydroplane sits in a cockpit.

Pilots wear jumpsuits that help them float in the water. They also wear crash helmets to protect their heads.

RACING UNLIMITED HYDROPLANES

Unlimited powerboat racing pilots are top professionals. They understand the excitement and danger of racing. As many as twenty-four boats compete in a race. This is a lot of traffic for boats with no brakes.

A member of a rescue team assists a pilot after an accident.

With so many boats racing on the water, crashes happen in nearly every race. Rescue teams wait in boats near the shore. They race to the accident to rescue the pilot. Their quick responses help bring injured racers back to the shore for medical care.

GOING
to the Races

Fans of powerboat racing have plenty of races to see across the country. Races take place in every state. There are also international race circuits. Powerboat racing has categories and classes for every fan around the world.

RACE LOCATIONS

From Florida to Michigan, and from New York to Washington, boat races are held on lakes and rivers every week. Each racing category has different regional races. The Outboard Drag Racing circuit has sixteen regions around the country. A region can be made up of two, three, or four different states. During a racing season, racers gain points that help them get to other competitions. Late in the season, regional champions race against each other in national races. The winners of the national races become the national champions of a class.

Fans have many chances to see races from lake beaches and riverbanks. They check their newspaper's sports sections for racing locations in their regions. Also, the APBA has race locations and times listed on its Web site.

ON SHORE

For fans, race day is a day of excitement. Most racing circuits are run on lakes and rivers that are close to the shore. This allows the fans to be close to the racing action.

A day at powerboat races is much like a day at the beach. Fans bring picnic lunches and lawn chairs. Kids play with sand buckets and beach balls. Everyone sits in the sun on the shore and watches the high-speed racing on the water.

Hydroplanes race on circuits near the shore to give spectators an exciting view.

Fans have many places on the shore from which to watch the racing. Racecourses measure from 1 and 2 miles (1.6 to 3.2 km) around a track. The track is laid out with brightly colored buoys. So, there is plenty of room on the shore for fans to sit and watch the races!

MEETING THE RACERS

Most race days are all-day events. Before and after the races, many powerboat pilots meet

with their fans. As race drivers do, powerboat racers have many fans.

Race days are as much for the fans as they are for the racers. There are areas for fans to see the powerful boats up close where they can admire the designs of the boats. Boat manufacturers are usually present on race days. Most of these boat makers also sell family boats. They display their watercraft so that fans can look at the boats closely.

HAVING FUN

Being a fan of powerboat racing is all about having fun. The speed of racing and the thrill of competition bring people of all ages to the shores. Pilots line up their boats. Suddenly, a great roar fills the air. There's a spray of water...the race is on!

Powerboat racers like to sign autographs for fans.

buoys colored floats that show boats where to go during a race

catamarans boats that have two hulls

categories divisions of a group

cockpit where a pilot of a boat or an airplane sits

displacement the size of an engine that tells how powerful it is

endurance being able to last long

hydroplane to move just above the surface of the water

NEW WORDS

racing circuits groups of planned races that take place over several months

regions parts of a country

shaft a metal bar that connects an engine to a propeller

sponsors companies that pay racers to advertise their products

For Further READING

Burnhoft, Simon. *High-Speed Boats: The Need for Speed.* Minneapolis, MN: The Lerner Publishing Group, 1999.

Graham, Ian, and Tom Connell. *Boats, Built for Speed.* Chatham, NJ: Raintree Steck-Vaughn Publishers, 1998.

RESOURCES

ORGANIZATIONS
American Power Boat Association
17640 East Nine Mile Road
Eastpointe, MI 48021

Unlimited Hydroplane Racing Association
19530 Pacific Highway South, #200
Seattle, WA 98188

U.S. Offshore Racing Association
18 North Franklin Boulevard
Pleasantville, NJ 08232

RESOURCES

WEB SITES

American Power Boat Association

www.apba-boatracing.com

This site gives information about all classes of powerboat racing. There are action photos of top drivers and their boats. The site also includes regional race schedules and TV schedules.

Unlimited Lights Racing Series

www.ulrs.org

Learn about the history of Hydroplane racing at this site. See photos of all boats that race each year for the series championship. Learn how the fastest boats on water are designed and built!

INDEX

INDEX

About The Author
Mark Beyer is a writer and educator who lives in Florida.